The Peaches on the Beaches

A BOOK ABOUT INFLECTIONAL ENDINGS

Brian P. Cleary

illustrations by
Jason Miskimins

Consultant:
Alice M. Maday
Ph.D. in Early Childhood Education with a Focus in Literacy
Assistant Professor, Retired
Department of Curriculum and Instruction
University of Minnesota

M Millbrook Press/Minneapolis

to Mrs. Tama,
my sixth-grade and eighth-grade teacher
in Rocky River, Ohio
—B.P.C.

Millbrook Press
A division of Lerner Publishing Group, Inc.
241 First Avenue North
Minneapolis, MN 55401 U.S.A.

Website address: www.lernerbooks.com

Library of Congress Cataloging-in-Publication Data

Cleary, Brian P., 1959–
    The peaches on the beaches : a book about inflectional endings /
by Brian P. Cleary ; illustrations by Jason Miskimins ; consultant:
Alice M. Maday.
        p.   cm. — (Sounds like reading)
    ISBN 978-0-8225-7636-5 (lib. bdg. : alk. paper)
    1. English language—Suffixes and prefixes—Juvenile literature.
2. Reading—Phonetic method—Juvenile literature. I. Miskimins,
Jason, ill. II. Maday, Alice M. III. Title.
    PE1175.C53 2009
    428.1'3—dc22   2008012768

Manufactured in the United States of America
1 2 3 4 5 6 – BP – 14 13 12

Can you find three words that sound alike?

They took **naps** with **caps** on their **laps**.

snowing

blowing

towing

Can you find three words that sound alike?

It was **snowing** and **blowing** when the truck was **towing**.

dreamed

screamed

beamed

EEE!

EEE!

Can you find three words that sound alike?

8

He **dreamed** that he **screamed** as the sun **beamed**.

witches

switches

ditches

Can you find three words that sound alike?

The **witches** put the **switches** in the **ditches**.

stretches

sketches

fetches

Can you find three words that sound alike?

12

He **stretches** and **sketches**
as the dog **fetches**.

cried

dried

tied

Can you find three words that sound alike?

The tears that she **cried dried**
when her shoes were **tied**.

screeches

peaches

leeches

Mom **screeches** at the **peaches**
and the **leeches** on the **beaches**.

clocks

rocks

socks

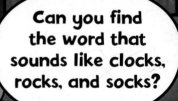

Can you find the word that sounds like clocks, rocks, and socks?

The **ox** by the **clocks** has **rocks** in his **socks**.

slacks

yaks

snacks

Can you find the word that sounds like slacks, yaks, and snacks?

The **racks** of **slacks** are by the **yaks** with the **snacks**.

mopped

dropped

shopped

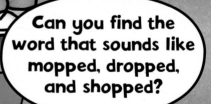

Can you find the word that sounds like mopped, dropped, and shopped?

The man **mopped** what she **dropped**
as we **stopped** and **shopped**.

cooks

books

hooks

Can you find the word that sounds like cooks, books, and hooks?

24

Dad **cooks** as Mom **looks** at the **books** by the **hooks**.

games

frames

flames

Can you find the word that sounds like games, frames, and flames?

We play **games** with our **names** as Dad throws the **frames** into the **flames**.

writing

fighting

biting

Can you find two words that sound like writing, fighting, and biting?

The **exciting writing** about fish **fighting** and **biting** was quite **inviting**.

braces

faces

vases

Can you find two words that sound like braces, faces, and vases?

They wore **braces** on their **faces** and brought **vases** in **cases** to the **races**.

Brian P. Cleary is the author of the best-selling Words Are CATegorical® series as well as the Math Is CATegorical® and Adventures in Memory™ series. He has also written several picture books and poetry books. In addition to his work as a children's author and humorist, Mr. Cleary has been a tutor in an adult literacy program. He lives in Cleveland, Ohio.

Jason Miskimins grew up in Cincinnati, Ohio, and graduated from the Columbus College of Art & Design in 2003. He currently lives in North Olmsted, Ohio, where he works as an illustrator of books and greeting cards.

Alice M. Maday has a master's degree in early childhood education from Butler University in Indianapolis, Indiana, and a Ph.D. in early childhood education, with a focus in literacy, from the University of Minnesota in Minneapolis. Dr. Maday has taught at the college level as well as in elementary schools and preschools throughout the country. In addition, she has served as an emergent literacy educator for kindergarten and first-grade students in Germany for the U.S. Department of Defense. Her research interests include the kindergarten curriculum, emergent literacy, parent and teacher expectations, and the place of preschool in the reading readiness process.

For even more phonics fun, check out all eight SOUNDS LiKE READiNG™ titles listed on the back of this book!

And find activities, games, and more at www.brianpcleary.com.

naps

caps

laps

Dear Parents and Educators,

As a former adult literacy coach and the father of three children, I know that learning to read isn't always easy. That's why I developed **Sounds Like Reading**™—a series that uses a combination of devices to help children learn to read.

This book is the seventh in the **Sounds Like Reading**™ series. It uses rhyme, repetition, illustration, and phonics to introduce young readers to inflectional endings. These include -s, -es, -ed, and -ing.

Starting on page 4, you'll see three rhyming words on each left-hand page. These words are part of the sentence on the facing page. They all feature inflectional endings. As the book progresses, the sentences become more challenging. These sentences contain a "discovery" word—an extra rhyming word in addition to those that appear on the left. Toward the end of the book, the sentences contain two discovery words. Children will delight in the increased confidence that finding and decoding these words will bring. They'll also enjoy looking for the mouse that appears throughout the book. The mouse asks readers to look for words that sound alike.

The bridge to literacy is one of the most important we will ever cross. It is my hope that the **Sounds Like Reading**™ series will help young readers to hop, gallop, and skip from one side to the other!

Sincerely,

Brian P. Cleary

Look for me to help you find the words that sound alike!